Absolute Crime Presents:

Made in USA

One Man's Dream to Manufacture Cheap Clothes...At All Costs

ABSO**|**UTE CR**|**ME

By Reagan Martin

Absolute Crime Books

www.absolutecrime.com

Table of Contents

About Us

Absolute Crime publishes only the best true crime literature. Our focus is on the crimes that you've probably never heard of, but you are fascinated to read more about. With each engaging and gripping story, we try to let readers relive moments in history that some people have tried to forget.

Remember, our books are not meant for the faint at heart. We don't hold back—if a crime is bloody, we let the words splatter across the page so you can experience the crime in the most horrifying way!

If you enjoy this book, please visit our homepage to see other books we offer; if you have any feedback, we'd love to hear from you!

PROLOGUE

'*Sweatshops*'- it's a word that conjures up dark images of small children sitting behind sewing machines, working long hours for very little pay, in dull and dirty factories. The word first originated in the mid 1800's to describe just those conditions, at a time when these factories flourished in such places as Great Britian and New York City. These places earned the name 'sweatshop' for the brutally hot conditions under which the employees were forced to work.

Throughout the years, many tragedies occurred in these sweatshops, but probably none more tragic than the fire that struck the Triangle Shirtwaist Factory in New York City on March 25, 1911. The factory occupied the top three floors of a ten story building in Greenwich Village near Washington Square Park. On that March day, managers had locked the exits and stairwells to prevent the employees from taking unauthorized breaks. Around 4:30 in the afternoon, a fire broke out and quickly turned into a raging inferno. With the stairwells and exits blocked, workers could not get out of the building. When they realized they were trapped, many of them began jumping out of the top floor windows. By the time the fire was brought under control, a total of 146 people had perished.

The fire finally brought attention to the sweatshops operating in the city, and legislation was quickly passed to ensure better safety standards in the workplace. It was also this incident that led to the formation of International Ladies Garment Workers Union which continues to fight for better working conditions to this day.

Little by little things improved for immigrants coming to both America and Great Britain, and sweatshops eventually came to be a thing of the past, although this does not mean that they no longer exist in places such as the U.S. and the U.K.

The word sweatshop is defined as 'working long hours for low pay in below standard conditions' so technically, those wealthy residents who hire illegal aliens to work in their homes and fields, for less than minimum wage, could be said to be operating 'sweatshops.' Although most people don't view them that way.

Those sweatshops that people envision when they hear the word do exist however, mostly in third world countries such as China, Vietnam and Thailand. Here, very young children, as well as men and women of all ages, are still employed to work long hours for extremely low pay.

It is an ongoing problem that most people attribute to nothing more than greed. But there are two views to every situation. While many support bringing an end to the sweatshops of the world, there are a surprising number of people who defend them. And they are not just the factory owners, but many of the people who work in them too.

Those who live in these third world countries toil long and hard anyway, and often for far less money than they can make in a sweatshop. In many respects, to lose these jobs in the factories would make their lives far more difficult.

For an American, to hear that a sweatshop worker was being paid .30 cents an hour for a 60 hour workweek, might sound like modern day slavery. But when one considers that the average pay for this same person in their own country is $1.00 a day, it doesn't sound so bad to be making $3.00 a day in a sweatshop.

In 1993 Tom Harkin, an Iowa Senator, proposed banning imports from any country that used children in sweatshops. This may have seemed like a wonderful idea, but as a result of it, the country of Bangladesh laid off 50,000 children. And, according to Oxfam, a leading British charity, a large number of these children were forced to become prostitutes in order to earn a living and survive.

It is for just these reasons that many people from poor countries still accept jobs in factories they know will be labelled sweatshops. They've heard the horror stories, but they're used to working long hours anyway, and for less pay, and in less than perfect conditions. They assume they might face harsher restrictions and less freedom, and they're willing too. In truth, they firmly believe it won't be all that much different from their current lives.

Of course, none of them had ever worked for Kil Soo Lee before, but that didn't matter. They were certain he wasn't operating a sweatshop anyway.

CHAPTER ONE

When 48-year-old South Korean Kil Soo Lee chose the Pacific island of American Samoa to house his new garment factory, it seemed, too many, like a dream come true. Lee portrayed himself as a kind and generous businessman, eager to hire those less privileged than himself. He wanted to offer hard-working people, those who struggled daily because of pitifully low wages, a new start at life.

The majority of Lee's work force would be made up of young females, comprised of Samoan, Vietnamese and Chinese nationals. Girls who would sew clothing - sporting attire, jackets, and swimsuits - at The Daewoosa Samoa Garment Factory LTD. These goods would then be exported to the United States, and other countries, to be sold in such stores such as JC Penney, Sears and Target.

Officials on American Samoa believed Lee's new factory would benefit both their residents, and their stagnant economy, and they were happy to have him. The country of Vietnam felt the same way.

Lee was promising his Vietnamese workers a monthly salary of $400, regardless if work was available for them or not. In a country where 80% of the population was made up of farmers who averaged an annual salary of just $200 per year, this was an astronomical amount of money. But for the Vietnamese hierarchy, there was an added bonus. They could charge their citizens a high fee just for the opportunity to work at the factory and for the documentation needed to leave their country.

For the government of Vietnam, it was a win/win situation. Potential employees could be charged $3,000 to $8,000 to secure the job, guaranteeing the government a huge profit on this fee alone, and of course once the person was actually working, most of their pay would undoubtedly be sent back home where it would quickly be introduced into the country's struggling economy. How could the Vietnamese government lose?

But it wasn't just American Samoa and Vietnam that were happy about the situation, the United States was pleased with it as well. Just like Puerto Rico, American Samoa, which is located 2300 miles south of Hawaii, is an unincorporated territory of the United States. It is not a state, nor are its residents considered American citizens, but the little island shares a close relationship with its parent country. Although the Samoans cannot vote in U.S. elections, its government is modeled after America's, and they have an elected delegate to the U.S. Congress. In addition, any elected President to the United States automatically becomes the head of state on American Samoa.

Because of these close ties, a factory on the island could be of great benefit to the U.S. Materials used in the manufacture of the clothing could be sent directly from the mainland, thereby enabling the factory to create stateside standard clothing which could then carry the 'Made in the USA' label. And because of the cost efficiency of creating the garments on the island, where the minimum wage was half of that in the states, the U.S. would be able to sell the clothing at highly competitive prices. Also saving thousands of dollars was the fact that goods made in American Samoa are not subjected to U.S. import quotas and tariffs.

All in all, the new Daewoosa Samoa Garment Factory seemed to be a great thing for people everywhere. When it opened its doors for business in 1998, hundreds of people had high hopes that it would change their lives forever. Unfortunately, they were right.

****

Dung Nguyen was a young, pretty Vietnamese girl, married and living with her husband and small daughter, when she first heard about the wonderful job that paid such good wages. Her next door neighbor brought an advertisement to show her, and as Dung read it, she thought it sounded almost too good to be true. A factory job in America, offering free room and board, plus a salary of $100 a week whether work was available or not? Dung simply couldn't believe it.

But it was obvious her neighbor believed it as she chattered on enthusiastically, thrusting the advertisement into the young girl's hands. Dung listened quietly to what her friend had to say, but she remained skeptical. She had heard horror stories of people taking 'fabulous' jobs, only to end up working in a 'sweatshop,' thousands of miles from home. Dung had no desire to become employed in one herself.

But her neighbor scoffed at her worries. "Not here," she said, "this job is in America. There are no sweatshops there."

Dung took the advertisement home and later that night she and her husband sat down to discuss it. Although both knew that there were pro's and con's to the job, each agreed it was certainly an opportunity worth considering. The money was exceptional, and the chance to work in America was like a dream come true. In America, even the poorest of people seemed rich too most.

But the job required a guarantee of three year's work from anyone interested in taking it, and Dung would have to leave her young daughter and husband behind. That was a long time for her to be away, living all alone in a strange country, and she worried about the sacrifice her husband would be making too. Their roles would have to be reversed; while she worked, he would have to stay home to care for their only child.

Although there was a lot to consider, the young couple found themselves relegating the cons to the bottom of the list. They found it difficult to move past the lure of such good money, and the more they spoke about it the more excited they became.

Further inquiries put a damper on things however, when Dung learned that she would have to pay a fee before taking the job, and a hefty fee at that. The price for her to go to work in America would cost Dung and her family $6,000. Money the Nguyen's simply did not have.

But even this was easily remedied, the Vietnamese labor officials told them. They could borrow the money from family, friends, or even a bank, and if that didn't work out there were always 'wealthy' people willing to help. Although the actual word for these wealthy people was never used, the Nguyen's were well aware that the officials were talking about loan sharks.

For almost a week, the young couple fretted over what they should do, and in the end they decided the job was simply too good to pass up. Just the chance to work and live in the United States was worth more than they could put a price on, and although they would miss each other, they felt the time would pass quickly.

Reasoning that over the course of the three years, Dung would earn a minimum of $14,400 - and possibly a lot more if she were able to take on other part time work during her off hours at the factory – both she and her husband believed that any sacrifice would be worth the reward. With that kind of money, even after paying back the initial fee, they would still see a profit of 8 to 10 thousand dollars. At Vietnamese wages, it might take them more than 40 *years* to earn that kind of money. With their decision finally made, Dung made preparations to leave for America, and others all over her country were doing the same.

Vietnamese job recruiters had offered 36-year-old Hoang Trong Thuy and his 33-year-old wife Nguyen Thi Ngoc, the chance to earn a staggering $36,000 for only three years' work at the Daewoosa Garment Factory in 'America.' Blinded by such a lucrative opportunity, just as so many others were, the couple quickly made arrangements to leave their four children behind and borrowed $11,000 from loan sharks to secure the job.

Throughout Vietnam, more than 200 people made the same decision, and none of them were unaware of the risks they took to do so. They borrowed money from family, friends and loan sharks, with no guarantee that they would ever be able to pay it back, and they willingly left behind everything that ever mattered to them. It was undeniable proof of just how bad things were in their own country.

Although it was a scary time for everyone, those who left were infused by an indomitable spirit and a burning desire to improve their lot in life. Things *would* work out, they assured themselves. They were travelling to the United States after all, where they would live and work in idyllic conditions and earn a small fortune. They were happy and excited by the opportunity, and despite all the risks, they truly believed it would all be worth it.

****

On the day Dung Nguyen was to travel to her new job in the United States, she dressed herself carefully, in a white blouse and new blue jeans, and packed her belongings in a small plastic suitcase. She not only wanted to look nice for her trip, but she wanted to look like an American.

At the airport, she kissed her husband and daughter goodbye, and then boarded the plane that would take her to her new job, and a brighter future for her family. The plane touched down in Honolulu Hawaii, where Dung boarded a second plane in a connecting flight. Later that day, she arrived at her destination, the island of American Samoa, 5,000 miles from her home and family.

As Dung exited the plane, she still believed that she had arrived in the United States, but she began to worry almost immediately. Why was the airport so small and empty, she wondered? It seemed odd because she had seen pictures of the massive airports in the U.S., and they always appeared to be jammed with mobs of rushing people. The weather wasn't what she expected either. Stepping outside of the air-conditioned building, the hot, sticky, humid heat assured Dung that she was still in the tropics and not in North America.

There was a bus waiting to take the women out to their new job at Daewoosa Garment Factory, and Dung climbed aboard, noticing the puzzled expressions on her fellow travelers and new co-workers. It seemed obvious that their final destination had not met their expectations either.

Reaching the factory, Dung saw a huge warehouse style building made of corrugated metal with a shiny tin roof. The blazing sun, which glared off of it, blinded her and hurt her eyes. All around the building, encircling the entire compound, was a high fence topped by razor wire in several sections. There was a guard shack at the entrance, and Dung could see a man's glaring face peering out at them. It reminded her of a maximum security prison, and she was instantly afraid.

When she was led into the warehouse and up to her dormitory, Dung's heart sank. The place looked like a barn with too many people haphazardly shoved inside. The smell was stomach turning; a combination of human waste, moldy clothing, and body odor. Strung all across the room were clotheslines with shirts, pants, socks and underwear hanging from them. The air was thick, heavy and sweltering. Sweat pour off people's faces and saturated their shirts. Rodent feces covered the floors and the beds, an inch or more thick in places. There were no screens on any of the windows, and the place literally buzzed with bumping insects floating about. There were no sinks, no hot water, no soap, and no toilet paper in sight. A dilapidated and disgustingly filthy shower stood in one corner of the room.

Dung stood frozen in place, drinking in the sight. She wanted to turn and run, to flee back to Vietnam and her husband and daughter. But she had already been warned that if she quit or left, or got herself deported, she would be fined an additional $5,000. She realized that the entire thing had been a fraud, a scam, a misrepresentation. She had been reluctant to apply because of the horror stories she had heard about sweatshops, and now it looked like she was going to be living in one.

Finally, Dung spoke. "Is this where we're going to live?" She asked in a trembling voice.

The man who had escorted them up to the dormitories gave her a little shove.

"Of course." He answered coldly, turning around to leave.

When he was finally gone, the other female workers approached Dung. This was a ritual they went through every time new arrivals appeared. They knew the girls who came had been duped, just like they had been duped when they first came, and they offered what little comfort they could. Dung looked so tiny, and so terrified, that the others finally offered her what they considered the dormitory's best bed. It was a top bunk, with a thin foam mattress, and they brought her a small wooden box to keep her belongings in. The bunk was considered the best because Dung would be allowed to sleep in it alone, as most of the women slept two to a bed, but more so because it was up high. Up there, the rats that came every night to chew through the women's mattresses and clothing, wouldn't be able to reach her.

Dung climbed up onto her bunk and began to cry. She was weary and exhausted after her long trip, but it was still several hours before she dozed off.

CHAPTER TWO

For two full weeks Dung sweltered in the dormitory with nothing to do. She didn't know why she wasn't put to work, but she wished she had been. Being alone with her thoughts, feeling nauseous from the stench that emanated throughout the building and permeated the very clothes everyone wore, Dung found herself utterly miserable; and scared, very, very scared. She was hearing horror stories about the Daewoosa Factory that she found hard to believe.

She learned that although the workers were allowed to leave the fenced in compound once their shifts ended, they had a 10:00 pm curfew, and woe be it to anyone who broke curfew. If you were late coming back you were either slapped, beaten or abused. You were searched each time you left the factory and each time you returned, and often personal items were confiscated and never returned. At other times, if the owner was concerned about something, the factory would go on lockdown and no one was allowed to leave.

She was told not to count on anything that had been promised to her before she came here. They were supposed to work an eight hour day and get paid overtime for anything beyond 40 hours a week, but that never happened. Sometimes they were forced to work 18 hour workdays for a month or more, and then would be given no work for weeks at a time. They were never paid for this either, even though they had been assured they would be paid whether work was available or not.

Dung also learned very quickly to be careful when taking a shower in her dormitory. The first day she did, she found herself standing ankle deep in a pool of human feces, and even more startling, her boss stood outside the stall, leering at her naked body. The toilets constantly backed up into the showers, and the factory owner, along with several of the guards, regularly watched the young women as they took showers and got dressed.

Although Daewoosa Factory employed Vietnamese, Chinese and Samoan nationals, of the 313 employee's there, 251 were Vietnamese, and 90% of all the workers were women. They had all come to this place with the same hopes and dreams and excitement, and each of them had those feelings shattered in an instant.

Dung was allowed to write letters home, and make phone calls when she was outside the compound, and she wrote to her family all the time. She told them how much she missed them, and how much she loved them, but she was careful not to reveal how truly awful things were for her. She didn't want to burden them with any added worry. She figured they were probably worried enough already.

After two weeks, Dung was brought into the factory and placed behind a sewing machine. The work came non-stop, and it was so stifling hot in the huge metal building that the temperature soared to 100 degrees and beyond. The constant running of the machines added to the heat, and contributed to the stench already hanging heavy in the air. Now, added to the aroma of human waste and body odor was the cloying smell of oil and exhaust.

Guards armed with plastic pipes zigzagged through the plant, patrolling it, and continually shouting at the workers.

"Faster, go faster!" The guards screamed. If they didn't feel someone was working at their full capacity, they would strike out with their pipes, hitting and beating the women like cattle being urged to move quicker.

But the guards were not the workers only problem. There was also Kil Soo Lee. The plant owner would visit the factory floor on a regular basis, urging the guards to hit certain workers, and repeatedly telling them not to worry if they killed them because he would take full responsibility for it. When he wasn't ordering beatings, Lee was busy groping the women, squeezing their breasts, patting their buttocks, and rubbing his hands between their legs. Several times Lee would order women off the floor and take them away. When they returned, the women would be crying and upset, a look of shame evident on their faces. Many would later admit that their boss had forced them to have sex with him.

The work days were long, and the atmosphere on the factory floor was one of terror and despair. The workers were given barely anything to eat, and what they did receive was almost inedible. Kil Soo Lee fed all 313 employees on little more than three or four heads of cabbage boiled in water with a little musty rice thrown in for good measure. Only very rarely were they treated to a small bowl of chicken casserole.

As a result of these meager rations, everyone in the factory began losing weight at a rapid pace. Most were tiny Asian women to begin with, girls who couldn't afford to lose weight anyway. But that didn't matter, each of them got thinner and thinner until the factory looked like it was housing nothing more than a bunch of walking skeletons. After a while, many of the women were so malnourished and abused that they quit getting their monthly menstrual cycles. Everyone at Daewoosa, men as well as women, quickly became weak and frail within the first few months of arriving.

Beatings were one form of punishment, but starvation was another. Even though none of the employees got enough to eat, there were times when certain ones were denied any food for days at a time. Despite being in this weakened condition, the employees knew not to let their work load decrease or they risked a beating on top of their starvation.

The workers lived under constant threats of arrest, jail, and deportation, not to mention the $5,000 fine they would incur if they quit or broke the contract. Most couldn't have left even if they wanted to because Kil Soo Lee immediately confiscated all passports as soon as the workers arrived.

Sometimes, when it was too suffocating to stay inside, the workers would go outside to try and catch a breeze inside the enclosed fence of the compound. One Samoan man who lived nearby would find his heart breaking every time he saw the young women out there. Although he and others could never have imagined how truly awful things were for the Daewoosa workers, they were aware that they didn't have it easy inside those locked gates. The whole bunch of them appeared to be starving to death, and many of the women would cry at the fence begging for food. At other times, when the workers were allowed outside the factory gates, the islander's would see them in town ravaging through garbage cans looking for something to eat.

The Samoan man who lived nearby could not afford to feed the group, but he did try to make their life a little more bearable. Often, he would drive his truck over to the compound and park just outside of the fence. There, he would set up a movie screen in the bed of his pick-up truck, and using a movie projector he would show films to the mass of workers milling around outside. The man would stare at the workers as they watched the movie, and each time he did, he was reminded of pictures he had seen from WWII. To him, the workers looked just like Germany's Jews, with their gaunt and sad faces sitting atop emancipated bodies, peering out from behind the concentration camp fences.

****

Kil Soo Lee robbed his workers blind from the moment they began working for him. The minimum wage in American Samoa was $2.60 per hour, totaling a monthly salary of $460.00. Yet the most Lee ever paid anyone was $195.00 a month, and many of those who worked for him were paid nothing at all. If the workers questioned the amounts in their paycheck, Lee would explain that he had to deduct $200 a month for room and board, despite the fact that they had been told this would be free before they came. If they continued to question it, their inquiries would be met with a slap in the face or a hit from a plastic plumbing pipe.

The workers were despondent and afraid. Many had borrowed huge sums of money to come here, and now their families were left back home to deal with the consequences. Loan sharks were calling in loans, and some were threatening to take away people's houses if the money wasn't paid. Their families had no money to pay the debts, and the workers now had none to send to them.One evening after leaving the compound and going into town, several young female workers had come across the Seafarers Center, a shelter run by Christian missionaries in the city of Pago Pago. The center staff was kind to them and gave them some food to eat.

On the evening of Sunday, March 28, 1999, five of these girls returned to the center crying and upset, and begging for help. The girls did not speak English, and communicating was difficult for the center staff, but they were able to get the gist of what the girls were trying to tell them. They were hungry, the girls said, and had not eaten since Friday, two days earlier.

The missionaries fed the frightened Vietnamese, and tried to interpret what the girls so desperately wanted to tell them. From what they could gather, being deprived of food was a common punishment at the factory, and the workers stayed because they had no way leave. Not only had their employer confiscated everyone's passports but, despite the fact the girls had been working there since 1998, none of them had received any money at all.

Captain Rob Stip, an American missionary, on the island with his wife and son, was appalled by the girl's story and immediately called the U.S. Embassy in Washington D.C. The girls spoke to someone first, and then Stip got on the line with an Embassy official. When he finally hung up, the captain asked the Vietnamese if they could return the next day and bring a copy of the contract they had signed before coming to American Samoa. The girls agreed, and then quickly left the center.

But the next day, as Captain Stip waited for the girls to arrive, he received a call from an unidentified female saying the girls would not be coming because the factory was on lockdown. Later in the afternoon, around 5:30 pm, Stip received a second phone call, this time from a crying young girl who pleaded with him to come to the factory at once. Although the captain didn't know what was going on, he agreed to drive out there but decided to take another staff member, Kevin Moushon, with him.

When the two men arrived at the factory, they saw three or four girls sitting inside the security gate, several guards standing around them. As soon as the guards saw Stip and Moushon walking towards them, they began beating the helpless girls, hitting and kicking them brutally, as they pled for mercy and tried to ward off the blows.

Stip and Moushon were stunned by the savagery, and then they saw something that shocked them even more. Rushing towards the fence, covered in blood and bruises, were approximately 30 more young Vietnamese girls. Each of them were crying hysterically, and begging the two men to help them.

Stip and Moushon stared at each other for a moment, confused and baffled, and then the captain demanded to know what was going on.

But the guards refused to answer, and instead started beating the girls again, hitting, slapping, kicking and punching as the terrified workers tried to crawl away to escape the abuse. No one seemed to notice the big shiny car pull up and the large Samoan man exit it.

Moving to stand between the two men and the fence, the man glared at Stip and Moushon, and then identified himself as an attorney representing the Daewoosa Garment Factory. He ordered the men to leave immediately and threatened to call the police if they didn't.

A furious Captain Stip told the attorney to go ahead and call the police, as he had no intention of going anywhere until he was told why the girls were being beaten.

The attorney called Stip's bluff and within minutes police officer David Snow arrived. He tried to calm things down and then, incredibly, he ordered the two men to leave the premises immediately. Stip and Moushon began to protest, trying to explain to the officer what was happening to the young girls, but Snow cut them off. He had already spoken to the factory owner, Kil Soo Lee, Snow told them, and he had explained everything. The girls were 'hysterical' Lee claimed, because he had punished them by withholding their food. He denied that he had every abused the girls, or 'watched them dress or take a shower.'

Stip and Moushon stared at the officer open-mouthed. Who had said anything about watching the girls dress or take a shower, they wondered? Just what in the hell was actually going on in this factory? But neither man got the opportunity to ask any questions. Officer Snow insisted they leave right now or he was going to arrest both of them. Stip and Moushon felt they had little choice. They couldn't help anyone if they were sitting behind bars so the two men reluctantly departed from the factory.

Both Captain Stip and Kevin Moushon returned to the Seafarers Center angry, upset and worried. Worse yet, Stip and his family were scheduled to fly back home to North Carolina that very evening, and would not be returning for an entire month. The captain hated to go, especially now, but the plans had already been made and the plane tickets bought weeks ago. There was not much he could do about it.

Kevin Moushon was left in charge of the center during the Captain's absence, and two days after Stip returned home, he received a call from him. Moushon told him that one of the girls from the factory had run away and was at the center now.

"What should I do?" Moushon asked.

Stip wasn't sure what he should tell him. After the fiasco with Officer Dave Snow he certainly wasn't going to suggest he call the police. Nor did he think the girl should return to the factory, where he feared she might be killed this time. Captain Stip felt agitated and useless. He was 10,000 miles away, how was he supposed to know what to do?

Finally, the Captain told Moushon to give the girl refuge and help her in any way he could. He didn't know what else to say.

****

One week after Captain Stip left American Samoa, two more Daewoosa workers showed up at the Seafarers Center in the wee hours of the morning. This time it was two young Vietnamese men who were fluent in English. The men had risked their lives to leave, having snuck out of the compound and scaled the razor wire fence after hearing about the center from some of the other workers.

This time, those at the center heard the entire story of life behind the locked gates of the Daewoosa Garment Factory and the poor workers who were at the mercy of Kil Soo Lee. They listened in shocked silence as the story tumbled out of the two terrified men.

They heard about beatings and abuse, threats of arrest and deportation, the confiscated passports, starvation, and the fear those locked inside lived with every day. They were told of women being sexually harassed and raped, of 18 hour work days for little or no pay, of filthy and unsanitary conditions, and of Samoan guards who brutalized the workers.

It was a shocking story indeed, but not that surprising. Those at the center had not forgotten the other terrified workers, or what Captain Stip and Kevin Moushon had seen. The center was run by missionaries, Christian people who had dedicated their lives to helping others. Each of those working there knew that something needed to be done to help the workers at the Daewoosa Garment Factory.

So once again workers at the Seafarer Center placed a call to the U.S. Embassy, but this time they placed a second call as well, to a local civil rights attorney living on the island.

The two workers met with the lawyer and once again repeated their story of life at the factory. After much discussion, and some investigation, the attorney convinced a handful of workers to file a civil suit against Kil Soo Lee for their back wages.

Finally, the lawsuit was enough to bring some attention to the factory, and in May the U.S. Department of Labor, (DPL), and the National Labor Relations Board, (NLRB), began an investigation of the South Korean factory owner.

The suit was met with displeasure from both the Vietnamese and the American Samoan governments. It was embarrassing, and brought attention to each that they didn't want. On American Samoa, it also threatened to harm their tourism trade.

But no one was as unhappy as Kil Soo Lee, who was absolutely irate about the whole thing. He ordered his workers to drop their cases against him, but it was already too late. Even if his employees did agree to drop the case, the United States government was already involved, and everyone knew that although the wheels of government might turn slowly, once they were in motion they were almost impossible to stop.

Lee had other problems he was dealing with at the same time. He was upset to find that the lawsuit seemed to infuse his workers with courage they had not previously shown. They were calling their families, and smuggling letters of complaint out of the factory to mail to them. One girl had sent her father a heartbreaking letter of life on American Samoa, and the foolish man had actually gone to the Vietnamese authorities over it.

The girl's father had first visited the Ministry of Education Works and then the State Department, who in turn had sent him to the director of Tourism. The Vietnamese reaction to this 'troublemaker' at the Daewoosa Factory is evidenced by the father's reply to his daughter:

'We were reprimanded, [by the director of tourism], *'*the man wrote. *'There I was told you and 16 other workers went on strike for something about wages being early or late, I don't know. Why would you do that to bring shame on our family? I feel if you do not work according to the terms you and I have signed with the company, I am afraid you will be a pawn on the chessboard. On the other hand, you should not think the other 16 workers are all good people. Who knows, maybe they need to eliminate a pawn? About your life, I implore you to obey the leadership and the organization. There is no other way.'*

But the civil suit had shaken Lee, and he was beginning to fear that he might lose complete control of his workers. The last thing he needed was more attention being focused on his factory. He began keeping the Daewoosa compound on lockdown more often than not these days.

Frightened as he might be, when the DPL completed their investigation and levied fines against him in the amount of $755,000, Lee still chose to ignore them. Publicity of not, Kil Soo Lee was loath to part with any of his money. When the DPL also ordered him to start paying back wages owed to his employees, Lee pled poverty, claiming he had no money to do so.

If he was worried about defying the United States government, he didn't show it. In fact, Lee acted as if nothing had happened, and things continued at the Daewoosa factory just as they had always been. When no repercussions were forthcoming after his failure to comply with the DPL and NLRB demands, Lee relaxed even more.

Although the DPL would have liked to shut the Daewoosa factory down and put Kil Soo Lee out of business, they had no authority to do so. And when the factory owner failed to pay his workers the back wages that were owed them, the DPL and the NLRB issued his employees the checks themselves.

On the very day his workers received those checks, some in the amount of $2500 and more, Kil Soo Lee confiscated each and deposited them into his personal checking account. Any worker who balked at turning the money over was immediately scheduled for deportation.

When he took these checks to the American Samoan bank, Lee paid a visit to a loan officer and attempted to bribe him into authorizing a $500,000 loan he had recently applied for.

Nothing had come of the investigations and the lawsuit, and Lee's legal troubles seemed to be behind him. But the anger he harbored over what his workers had done was just beginning. From that moment on, conditions in the factory grew even worse. The beatings increased, and the workers were watched more closely. The compound was often on lockdown now and no one was allowed to leave. Lee had no intention of letting anyone else seek help at any shelters. The workers were absolutely miserable, and at night they sobbed in their sleep. One woman would later say about this time; "It sounded like everyone was going insane."

****

The factory workers considered the civil suit a failure, and were depressed that little seemed to come from it, other than harsher living conditions. They had no idea that, although it might have appeared to generate little publicity for them, behind the scenes it had gotten things moving. The suit brought the plight of the workers to the attention of the U.S. government and the people on American Samoa. And by the end of the year, the internet would bring it to the attention of the entire world.

One person who read about what was happening at the garment factory on the South Pacific Island was Hai-Tri Le, a Vietnam War refugee living in the United States. Le had made a good life for himself after the war, settling in the Seattle Washington area and securing an impressive position with The Microsoft Corporation. He was appalled by what he was reading and hearing concerning his fellow countrymen on American Samoa, and he was determined to help them in any way he could.

Someone else who was keeping an eye on what was happening on American Samoa was Representative Chris Smith, a Republican from the state of New Jersey. One of Smith's key aides had lived on the island and was familiar with the factory. Smith was a real humanitarian who was sickened by today's world of human trafficking and modern day slavery. He had been working tirelessly on ways to end these despicable practices, and he would eventually be the prime sponsor in getting the Trafficking Victims Protection Act passed later that year. It was a law that would play a big part in the fate of Kil Soo Lee, but it wouldn't prevent one of the most vicious occurrences from happening at his factory.

CHAPTER THREE

Shortly after the Human Trafficking Victims Protection Law was passed on October 28, 2000, the Daewoosa Samoa Garment Factory received a large order from JC Penney. The order was on a time limit, and needed to be completed within a month. Rush orders were always daunting tasks, and they always raised the stress level in the factory considerably, but Kil Soo Lee was determined to fulfill this one.

Things had been tense at Daewoosa for months. Between the legal troubles, the passing of the anti-trafficking law, and now the pressure of fulfilling this rush order, it seemed everyone's nerves were frazzled. Kil Soo Lee was stressed, the Samoan guards who prowled the factory floors were anxious, and the weary workers were apprehensive.

On November 28, 2000, despite the fact that it was late fall, the weather on the island of American Samoa was brutal. The sun was blazing hot, the air heavy with humidity, sticky, cloying, and nearly suffocating. Inside the corrugated metal confines of the Daewoosa Garment Factory, the temperature soared to 104 degrees. The workers sweated heavily, their hair and clothing so wet with perspiration they might have just stepped out of a shower.

The guards zigzagging amongst the workers, glaring menacingly and keeping their plastic pipes at the ready. All of the guards were Samoan, but not all of them were men. Lee often used female guards as well, and they could be every bit as vicious as their male counterparts. But the females were not employed for security, most were workers on the line who would only be pulled from their machines when needed.

On this day, the 30 guards roaming the factory floor were all men, each weighing between 200 and 300 pounds, and the tension in the room was palpable. The pressure to fulfill the JC Penney contract, combined with the stifling conditions inside the building, had everyone feeling more stressful and miserable than ever.

Daewoosa Samoa was fashioned in an assembly line, with each article of clothing moving from worker to worker, as different alterations were made. Those at the beginning of the line started immediately, but those at the end had no work until the assembly line began to move steadily.

Dung Nguyen sat next to 21-year-old Truong Thi Le Quyon, another Vietnamese seamstress who occupied the sewing machine next to hers. Dung was not feeling well. The heat, combined with the lack of food, made her feel weak and faint. The two women were at the end of the line, sitting at their sewing machines, waiting for the work to reach them.

Lee was on the floor too, urging his workers to move faster, shouting at them continuously. Dung watched as one of the Samoan guards approached her and Truong and began screaming at them about 'not working.' Truong tried to explain that the assembly line had not yet reached them, but the guard would not be pacified. Soon, Kil Soo Lee had moved over to the small group and joined his guard.

The two women were trying to explain the situation, but Lee and the guard were hearing none of it. Suddenly, the guard grabbed Truong by the hair and pulled her from her chair. He wrapped his massive hands around her delicate neck, and began squeezing the life out of her. Dung, thinking he would kill the woman, began to scream. She watched as Truong's eyes bulged in terror, and saw her face turn from pink to red to blue. Other workers stopped to stare at the altercation, some of them beginning to rise from their own seats.

Two Vietnamese men rushed to the guard and tried to interfere, and then, according to Dung, "it all happened." The guard released his grip on Truong long enough to begin clubbing the Vietnamese men with his plastic pipe. When other guards hurried over and took over the beating, the original guard turned back to Truong who was lying on the floor gasping for air. Immediately, he began beating on her, striking her in the head and the body, as she tried to pull herself into a fetal position.

Kil Soo Lee stood among them, smiling with glee and screaming at the top of his lungs. "Don't worry if you kill her," he shouted, "I'll take the blame for it."

The guard, egged on by his boss, grabbed Truong around the neck again and began dragging her towards the factory doors. He pulled her between the rows of the assembly line, leaving a trail of blood in his wake, as the other workers shouted for him to stop.

Suddenly, one Vietnamese man, Nguyen Thai Quang ran towards the two and grabbed hold of Truong, trying to pull her back. Other guards descended on him, clubbing him in the face and head, knocking out several of his teeth, and rupturing his eardrum. Other workers came to his rescue, but they were assaulted themselves, and soon the entire factory floor was in an all-out brawl.

There was fighting and screaming and yelling between everyone. Over and over again the guards raised their plastic pipes and brought them down on the Vietnamese and Chinese workers. Blood sprayed the entire factory, landing on the floor, the machines, and the garments, covering everything with a layer of crimson gore.

Outside the factory doors there was more fighting. The guard had managed to get Truong outside, but other Vietnamese had followed him, and other guards had followed them. There was an entire melee inside and out. Sialavaa Fagaima, a sometime seamstress who also worked as a security guard in the factory, picked up a plastic pipe and began swinging herself.

Fagaima hit and clubbed and beat any worker who came within range. So violently did she swing that she shattered the pipe she was holding, leaving its end jagged and splintered, turning it into a sinister and deadly weapon. Soon, Fagaima turned her lethal pipe onto Truong. She beat the woman mercilessly about the face and head, until one of those splintered ends caught the terrified woman perfectly at the corner of her eye. The jagged piece of plastic continued to move, gouging into the eye socket, entering Truong's head, and bringing her eyeball out with it when Fagaima finally pulled it back.

The sight was like something out of a horror movie. The blood gushed profusely out of the open wound, and the eyeball, now triple the size it appears when resting in the eye socket, dangled down below Truong's face held fast by a bloody and grotesque vein attached somewhere deep within her head.

Truong began to scream and react, clasping her hands over her gushing eye socket she blundered forward in a blind panic of fear and pain. Every time she moved, she sprayed and showered the gathering crowd with droplets of scarlet colored blood. Finally, the sight of her seemed to wake everybody up and the fighting quickly came to an end. The guards were scared, it was obvious that this time the beatings had gone too far.

They carried the injured woman back inside, where the sight of her brought an immediate halt to the others fighting on the factory floor. The woman was covered with blood, and Dung could see that she was badly hurt. It looked like a massacre had taken place inside the building, with almost every inch of it covered in a fine red mist.

The workers were immediately ordered back to their dormitories where they huddled in groups, terrified and afraid. In all the confusion of the melee, several workers had managed to leave the compound and were in town calling their families, begging for help to get back home. Everyone wanted to leave American Samoa right then and there.

But there was little their families could do.

****

Back on the factory floor, those workers who were too injured to be sent to the dormitories, including Truong Thi Le Quyon and Nguyen Thai Quang, lay on the ground in a heap. Some of the guards were trying to help them, but Kil Soo Lee didn't seem concerned, in fact he seemed enraged. He had an order to fill, damn it, and he had thousands of dollars of ruined, blood covered garments, and no workers on the floor.

While the injured lay helpless, Kil Soo Lee ranted and raved for two entire hours before the guards finally convinced him that they needed to go for help. Only then did Lee allow his workers to be taken to a hospital. But he made sure that the hospital staff was told that the workers had begun to riot, and the injuries were 'accidents' that occurred while the guards were trying to protect themselves.

Later that night, Virginia Soliai, a manager in the factory, visited the workers in their dormitories and ordered them to back up the story. She insisted that they file false reports indicating that any injuries suffered were incurred as a result of self-defense.

****

Kil Soo Lee had finally calmed down and begun to assess his situation, and for the first time ever, the South Korean businessman was truly scared. He doubted he could sweep this incident under the rug as neatly as he had the civil suit and the DPL investigation, and he quickly began making plans to secure his future. During the month of December, Lee visited several banks on the island of American Samoa.

Kil Soo Lee had been right. This time, things would not be swept under the rug so easily, and on January 12, 2001, a Samoan court ordered the Daewoosa Garment Factory into receivership. The factory had been a lucrative business, having exported over 8 million dollars in goods during some months, but despite this fact, the receiver found the company's bank accounts with a balance of only $538.00. Lee's many visits to the banks had enabled him to withdraw hundreds of thousands of dollars in the days and weeks leading up to the receivership. It seemed apparent now that Daewoosa Samoa Garment Factory LTD was bankrupt.

****

For more than a year now, Hai-Tri Le, the Microsoft employee back in Seattle, had been trying to bring the plight of the Daewoosa workers into the public eye. He had contacted many organizations, including SOS Boat People and the National Labor Committee, two humanitarian rights groups, and everyone was just as concerned as him. But getting the public, or the government, to come forward and take a stand had not occurred.

Now, upon hearing about the latest happening at the factory, Hai-Tri Le decided he needed to do something drastic to bring attention to the horrors being perpetrated on the island of American Samoa.

In February, Le took a leave of absence from Microsoft, traveled to American Samoa, and infiltrated the factory. For ten days, he bunked in the men's dormitory and worked on the factory floor, documenting everything he saw, and heard, with notes and pictures taken on his digital camera.

When he finally returned home, Le and several others took their case to the public in full force. They had been pressuring the United States Department of Justice to do something about the factory since 1999, with no luck. But now, armed with evidence that could blow the entire scandal sky high, the FBI took notice. And in late February of 2001, they finally travelled to American Samoa and began an investigation.

But they had not moved fast enough. The Daewoosa fiasco had been tremendously embarrassing to the Vietnam government, and they were determined to keep their role in it from being made public. Because of the FBI's failure to become involved earlier, a Vietnam Labor Company Official was able to fly to American Samoa and pressure his people to return home, and several did.

On March 23, 2001, the FBI arrested Kil Soo Lee on American Samoa and charged him with involuntary servitude and false labor practices. The disgraced businessman was immediately flown to the state of Hawaii and placed in a jail cell to await trial.

Although the Daewoosa Samoa Garment Factory was officially closed down, its workers were allowed to remain in the dormitories where they lived alone and virtually penniless. They had no way to return home and most were too afraid to go anyway. Not only were they terrified of the retribution they might suffer because of their association with the factory, but they were still responsible for the large debts they had incurred and they had no way to pay them back.

While the ex-workers wondered what would become of them, they struggled to find a way to get food and survive. They roamed the towns knocking on stranger's doors, and asking churches and shelters for help. Many offered to work in exchange for food, and were grateful to accept any odd job; sewing, cleaning, babysitting and running errands.

Some of the Samoans residents were kind and generous, paying the workers well for their efforts. But others were more than happy to take advantage of the situation, promising to pay but never coming through with the money. It was a sad situation all around.

CHAPTER FOUR

If the former workers from the Daewoosa Factory were despondent over the circumstances that had befallen their lives, they would have been grateful to know they had a champion in their corner. Hai-Tri Le had been fighting for their cause for more than a year now, and his drive and determination to help his fellow countrymen was intense and furious.

Le had spent copious amounts of money, risked his life and his job, and rarely saw his family in his quest to save those who fell victim to Kil Soo Lee. It was he who was instrumental in involving other human rights groups to join in pressuring the justice department to act, and it was he who was still working with them.

The Justice Department finally informed Le that Vietnam had plans to repatriate their former Daewoosa workers, and intended to send an airplane to American Samoa to bring them home. Le feared that those who returned to Vietnam would face political retribution, and he inquired about the United States granting citizenship to the refugees. But the Justice Department was reluctant to offer residency to such a large number of people, and they told Le, tentatively, that they might be willing to grant sanctuary to 20 former workers if they agreed to testify against Kil Soo Lee.

Hai-Tri Le was confused and angry. The Justice Departments offer simply wasn't good enough. Le believed that all the former employees should be allowed to come to the United States since all of them had endured the same hardships and abuse, and he was not about to just let the matter rest. Joining forces with dozens of volunteers and a handful of attorney's, Le and his group fought to gain U.S. residency for every former factory worker.

The United States, Le claimed, could easily do this, and in fact, had an obligation to under the new 'T' Immigration Visa, which provided sanctuary to federal witnesses who helped prosecute human traffickers and smugglers. The publicity worked, and as the general public rallied behind Le and the others, the Justice Department finally agreed.

They would give residency to those immigrants who had suffered at the hands of Kil Soo Lee and his Daewoosa Factory, but there was still another problem. The department didn't have the staff to find homes, sponsors and airline tickets for the stranded immigrants. Le and the others were not discouraged however. If the Justice Department couldn't do it, they would do it themselves.

This may have been easier said than done though, once the group found out about the time crunch they were on. The Vietnamese plane was due to arrive on American Samoa in as little as two weeks. Those trying to help the former factory workers would have only 10 days to accomplish their mission.

Hai-Tri Le immediately took another leave of absence from Microsoft and got on the internet and the phones. He created websites, posting messages that read: Your Fellow Vietnamese Need Your Help! He and dozens of others made phone calls to attorneys, the Justice Department, travel agents, churches, shelters, and anyone else they could think of. Le's cell phone bill alone ran $3,000 for the month.

Within days, 600 people had volunteered to help. But time was running out, and now, when Le placed phone calls, he had no time for questions or explanations. His manner was abrupt and to the point.

"Can you take workers? How many? Do you know of any other jobs for them? Do you know of any place that would sponsor them? Shelter them? Help them? Are you a Church? A business? A philanthropist? What?"

Finally, when their time was up, Le realized that there were still many, many workers left on the South Pacific Island. But he had made a promise to these people, and he intended to keep it. Le, and two volunteers, purchased each of the former workers a one way ticket off of American Samoa themselves. The cost to these three individuals was a staggering $42,000, of which $25,000 was charged to Le's credit card alone.

Now, with airline tickets in hand, Le found there were other problems. Some of the Vietnamese didn't want to go, they wanted to return home. They missed their families, and many husbands were adamant that their wives come back. The women were crying, torn between what they should do. They wanted to be with their husbands, who were threatening divorce, a shameful fate for a Vietnamese woman, but they were afraid to go home. They vacillated on what they should do, frustrating everyone involved.

As bad as that was, Le found it even worse that some of the former workers could not be found. They were still living in the dormitories, and doing work for island natives and no one knew whether they were working or looking for wages that were owed to them. Le found out that many of the Samoans they worked for had promised to pay them at the airport, and when they didn't show up, the former workers went looking for them. One Vietnamese girl missed her plane because she was trying to hunt down people who owed her $10.00, despite the fact that her missed plane ticket had cost $800. Le would be thankful when everyone was finally standing upon U.S. soil.

Things were difficult for the former workers when they first reached America, but nowhere near as difficult as it was for those who were repatriated back to Vietnam. For them, life was unbelievably hard and cruel back in their own country. Creditors hounded them daily, and several ex-workers had to go into hiding to avoid them. Twenty families lost their homes to loan sharks when they couldn't repay their debts. Those who had worked at Daewoosa were constantly ordered to report to the police to answer questions about their experiences on American Samoa, and many couldn't find jobs because they were now ostracized by their fellow countrymen. They wrote heartbreaking letters to the United States government, pleading with them for help since their own government refused to do so.

A lot of people who had read about what they had experienced wanted to help, and many wrote letters on their behalf to the U.S. government too. A church in Hawaii held a fund raiser and took up a collection to purchase Truong Thi Le Quyen a new glass eye. Others contributed to help pay for the surgery it would take to have the eye implanted. Countless others would have liked to help, but they really didn't know what they could do.

****

In August, Kil Soo Lee was indicted on 22 counts including involuntary servitude, extortion, money laundering, false financial reporting and bribery of a bank official. Also indicted with him were four others: Virginia Soliai and Robert Atimalala, two factory supervisors accused of working in concert with Samoan officials to deport workers who complained, Elekana Nuuuli Ioane, another factory supervisor who was accused of carrying out the beatings ordered by Kil Soo Lee, and Sialavaa Fagaima, the security guard who gouged out Truong's eye. Each was charged with human trafficking among other things.

Before Lee's trial even began, Ioane and Fagaima both pled guilty to the charges leveled against them. Fagaima received a sentence of 4 years and 3 months, while Ioane received 5 years 10 months. Both expressed remorse for their actions at sentencing.

Fagaima, looking meek and docile as she cried before the court, told the Judge, "There has never been a day or a night when I have forgotten what I have done. I wish I could turn it back, but I can't."

Ione, whispering in a soft voice, simply told the court, "I just want to say sorry. What I did was wrong."

Kil Soo Lee, the man ultimately responsible for all of this, never showed any remorse or sorrow at all.

AFTERWORD

Kil Soo Lee went to trial on October 22, 2002 before U.S. District Judge Susan Oki Mollway in Honolulu Hawaii. Originally charged with twenty-two counts, by this time four of them had been dismissed, but Lee still faced the possibility of conviction on eighteen separate counts. Also being tried alongside him were Robert Atimalala, and Virginia Soliai.

Twenty-one former Daewoosa employee's testified to the mistreatment they were subjected to at the hands of the one-time respected businessman. Some of those who took the stand were former supervisors and guards who drastically downplayed their participation in the horrors that occurred in the factory. For four entire months the trial dragged on slowly, but on February 21, 2003 Kil Soo Lee was convicted on 14 of the 18 counts. The jury judged that he was guilty of conspiracy, extortion, money laundering and 11 counts of involuntary servitude. Robert Atimalala and Virginia Soliai were subsequently found not guilty.

Lee's sentencing was delayed repeatedly for several different reasons, including the firing of his one-time attorney. When he appeared in court with his lawyer on January 28, 2004, Lee appeared glassy-eyed and confused. His attorney asked for another delay, claiming that he could no longer communicate with his client. When Judge Mollway tried to speak to Lee and ask him questions, the former factory owner simply stared at her shaking his head. He didn't understand the proceedings he repeatedly told her.

The Judge, although skeptical of Lee's newfound stupidity, had little choice but to postpone the hearing. She ordered Lee to undergo a mental evaluation, and scheduled a new sentencing date of May 6, 2004. But it was not until more than a year later, on June 22, 2005, that Kil Soo Lee was finally sentenced for his part in the happenings at the Daewoosa Samoa Garment Factory. Lee received a total of 40 years in prison, and was ordered to pay 1.8 million dollars in restitution.

The former factory owner's attorney immediately appealed on the grounds that Lee should not have been tried on United States soil but instead in American Samoa. The high court however, ruled that American Samoa did not have the courts to try him, and that the United States had jurisdiction for these types of federal crimes.

Today, Lee is 63-years-old and remains behind bars. It is likely he will die in prison. His Daewoosa factory has been shut down and remains a sad embarrassment for the island of American Samoa.

A total of 272 former Daewoosa workers now live in the United States, thanks to hundreds of people like Hai-Tri Le. Although they are scattered throughout the U.S., several of the women live in the Seattle area. For some, it is a new life with a bright future, but for others, it is a sad and lonely existence.

Many of the single women have found new loves in America and are starting new families. Others were eventually reunited with husbands and children, who were left in Vietnam, when they also qualified for residency in the United States. For them, the future looks bright too.

But for many more, there remains only memories of past lives, and loneliness in a foreign country filled with strangers. To these women, those they love remain in Vietnam, either unable or unwilling to start a new life thousands of miles away. Dung Nguyen is one of them. She lives alone in Seattle, working twelve hours a day, six days a week. She welcomes the long hours; they keep her from thinking too much.

Hai-Tri Le keeps in touch with those he helped to rescue from American Samoa, and they dream of the day all the former factory workers will be reunited with their families. To the ex-Daewoosa employees, Le is a hero of the greatest kind.

The two Vietnamese men who scaled the fence at the factory and sought help from the Seafarer Center have completely vanished. The Samoan government has stated that the two were victims of a drowning accident, but former factory workers have denounced this explanation. Their whereabouts remain unknown.

JC Penney, and many of the other large department stores that purchased clothing from the Daewoosa Garment Factory, immediately canceled their contracts with the distributor who supplied them. All of the garments from the factory were eventually auctioned off.

Lawyers from American Samoa and the United States filed a lawsuit against Kil Soo Lee, and two Vietnamese Labor Offices, for the employees of the garment factory. Eventually, an American Samoa court awarded the former workers 3.5 million dollars in damages. But since Lee is bankrupt, and sitting in prison, none of his ex-employees have seen a dime, and they are not ever likely too. Many are fighting to have the Vietnamese government pay, since they were judged responsible along with Lee, but so far nothing has come of that either.

What happened at the Daewoosa Samoa Garment Factory was undoubtedly a tragedy, and the conditions its workers were forced to live in were brutal and cruel. But not more so than thousands of other 'sweatshops' operating throughout the world. Had Kil Soo Lee not chosen an American territory to open his factory, chances are good that it would still be in operation today.

Perhaps one day more attention will be focused on those who find themselves working and living in sweatshops, and stricter penalties enforced on those who operate them. But since human trafficking is an enterprise that generates 7 to 10 billion dollars in profit each year, the greed of many will most likely keep that from ever happening. For it is only when each and every country takes a stand against such modern day slavery that anything might be accomplished in the fight to end it.

BIBLIOGRAPHY

http://archives.starbulletin.com/2001/09/05/news/ story10.html

http://www.globallabourrights.org/reports?id=021 5

http://www.seattlepi.com/default/article/Chapter- 1-Servitude-in-American-Samoa- 1129763.php#page-3

http://www.justice.gov/opa/pr/2003/February/03_ crt_108.htm

http://www.nytimes.com/2002/05/10/opinion/swe atshops-under-the-american-flag.html

http://www.seattlepi.com/default/article/The-story-behind-the-story-1129932.php

http://www.seattlepi.com/default/article/Sentencing-delayed-for-garment-factory-owner-1135848.php

http://www.seattlepi.com/default/article/Chapter-4-Smiles-laughter-and-a-wedding-in-a-1130067.php

http://www.seattlepi.com/default/article/A-joyful-reunion-for-woman-who-escaped-cruelty-of-1134873.php

http://www.seattlepi.com/default/article/Acts-of-kindness-showered-on-sweatshop-workers-1130378.php

http://www.seattlepi.com/default/article/The-U-S-acted-too-slowly-some-say-1130042.php

http://www.seattlepi.com/default/article/Chapter-3-Dramatic-flurry-rescues-workers-1130041.php

http://www.seattlepi.com/default/article/Timeline-1130039.php

http://www.seattlepi.com/default/article/In-her-own-words-Christa-Lin-attorney-for-1129988.php

http://www.seattlepi.com/default/article/The-story-behind-the-story-1129932.php

http://www.seattlepi.com/news/article/In-her-own-words-Dung-Nguyen-1129766.php

http://www.seattlepi.com/default/article/In-his-own-words-I-implore-you-to-obey-the-1130056.php

www.dfat.gov.au/geo/american_samoa/american_samoa.brief.html

http://econlib.org/library/Columns/y2008/Powells
weatshops.html

http://www.ilr.cornell.edu/trianglefire/

www.mzi.com/pages/news.php?op=read&id=374
4

http://archive.starbulletin.com/2004/02/02/news/s
tory11.html

Northwest Florida Daily News 09/02/01

www.ingramcontent.com/pod-product-compliance
Lightning Source LLC
Chambersburg PA
CBHW070929290526
45795CB00001B/479